Just Handwriti
Cursive Handwriting Prog
3rd Class

GW00870980

educate.ie

Author: Tony Walsh
Editor: Susan McKeever
Design: Philip Ryan Graphic Design
Illustration: Tim Hutchinson
© 2012 Educate.ie, Castleisland, County Kerry, Ireland.
ISBN: 978-1-908507-17-4

Printed in Ireland by Walsh Colour Print, Castleisland, County Kerry. Freephone 1800 613 111.

Contents

Introduction

There are eight books in the Just Handwriting series; one for each class from Junior Infants to Sixth Class. The aim of the programme is to enable children to write fluently, comfortably, quickly and legibly. Handwriting is a form of communication and one on which we are often judged.

Remember the Four Ps: Preparation, Pencil Grip, Posture, Practice.

Preparation (Junior Infants to Second Class): The simple, fun 'Let's Get Ready!' exercises help to relax the child mentally and physically and enable them to focus on the planned activity. Encourage the child to draw or trace the 'Giant Sunglasses' before every writing activity. In time, it will become part of their work routine.

Pencil Grip: The correct pencil grip will lead to quick, fluent writing.

Posture: Good posture helps the writing stamina of the child.

Practice: The formation of each letter is clearly illustrated so the child will have a reference that shows him or her how to form each letter, especially if more than one stroke is involved. Handwriting is an essential skill that needs to be taught and fluency only comes with plenty of practice. Practice, practice, practice makes perfect and enables the child to become a confident writer.

Assessment

There is a self-assessment option at the bottom of each page. The child ticks the face that they feel applies to their completion of the page.

Individual Books

Junior Infants Book: This book focuses on the correct formation of all lowercase letters. The letters are pre-cursive (with 'tails') so that the child can progress naturally to cursive writing. This level also includes a supplementary copybook; this focuses on the formation of lowercase letters, and can be used at the teacher's discretion.

Senior Infants and First Class Books: These books focus on the correct formation of all uppercase letters as well as further practice in lowercase. The Senior Infants book includes a supplementary copybook, focusing on capital letters, that can be used at the teacher's discretion.

Second Class Book: In the Second Class book the width of the lines changes from 6mm to 5mm from Page 39 onwards in preparation for third class. All writing exercises are meaningful e.g. recipes, quiz-style questions and answers and interesting facts.

Third Class Book: This is the stage where children are introduced to cursive looped writing. They will discover that many of the lowercase letters are unchanged from those that have been taught already. Most of the remaining letters involve loops. Later in the year the capital letters are introduced.

Fourth Class Book: Now the children begin to write using a pen. An inexpensive cartridge pen with a fine-pointed nib or a fine-pointed fibre pen (not felt) is recommended. Under no circumstances should a biro or a ballpoint pen be used. In fact these types of pens should not be used for writing in any primary school class.

The Fifth Class Book: Lower and uppercase letters are repeated from Pages 3 to 11 to revise, reinforce and provide practice of correct letter formation. The most important writing rules are repeated throughout the book. Pupils should use the same pen suggested in the Fourth Class book. The contents of this book vary from facts, stories and poetry to dictionary exercises and legends.

The Sixth Class Book: Lower and uppercase letters from Pages 3 to 8 provide revision of letter formation. Once again the writing rules are repeated throughout the book. The first half of the book has blue and red lines; the second half of the book has double blue lines for 12 pages and 'copy' lines for the last 12 pages. Pupils are recommended to use the same type of pen as they used in Fourth and Fifth Class. There is a variety of material in this book – factual pieces, legends, riddles, stories and tongue twisters.

Patterns

Before we begin joined writing we have to practise writing patterns like these.

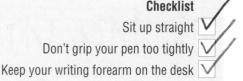

Patterns

The pattern on each line should be done without lifting the pencil.

(handwriting practice pattern rows)

Patterns

Do not lift the pencil until you have finished the pattern.

5

joins

We have to change some letters of the alphabet before we can join them. a, c, d, e, i, m, n, o, q, t, u and x do not change but we begin by making an up-stroke to them. All of them except 'o' finish with an up-stroke to the top blue line.

(handwriting practice rows of joined letters: iiii, inin, imim, nunu, imim, umum patterns)

Joins

Joins to a, c, d, q and o.
The up-stroke goes up, around and down to where these letters begin at the 'one o'clock' position.
The join from the 'o' to other letters is made by a curved line along the top blue line.

ccccccccc   aaaaaaaa   adadadad

ccccccccc   aaaaaaaa   adadadad

cccccccc   aaaaaaa   adaddad

ccccccc   aaaaaaa   adadadd

ccccccc   aaaaaaaa   adadada

dad   cad   dada   dac

dad   cad   dada   dac

dad   cad   dada   dac

dad   cad   dada   dac

o o o o o o o o o o

o o o o o o o o o o

o o o o o o o o o o

cod   moon   moan   cocoa

cod   moon   moan   cocoa

cod   moon   moan   cocoa

7

e

The up-stroke goes up and around to form the letter 'e'.

ie ue ne me ce de ee

ie ue ne me ce de ee

ie ue ne me ce de ee

ie ue ne me ce de ee

ie ue ne me ce de ee

nine men end dead dine

nine men end dead dine

nine men end dead dine

nine men end dead dine

nine men end dead dine

queen quad queue need

queen quad queue need

queen quad queue need

queen quad queue need

queen quad queue need

Joins to 't'.
The up-stroke goes to the top blue line and straight up to where the 't' begins. It comes down again and finishes at the top blue line. Do not cross the 't' until you have finished the word.

tttttttttttt tttttttttttt tttttttttttt

ttttttttttttttt ttttttttttttt

met date tame cute meat
met date tame cute meat

note dote toot quota to
note dote toot quota to

9

h

The up-stroke goes up and around to form a loop at the top red line. It then comes down to the bottom blue line, crossing the up-stroke at the top blue line. It then goes up and around to finish like an 'n'.

h h h h h h h h h h

h h h h h h h h h h

h h h h h h h h h

hand that then chin hate

hand that then chin hate

hunt home chum cheat hat

hunt home chum cheat hat

k

'k' begins like a 'h'. The up-stroke makes a loop at the top red line and comes down straight to the bottom blue line. It then goes up, around and in between the two blue lines. It comes out, down to the bottom blue line and finishes with an up-stroke.

k k k k k k k k k k

k k k k k k k k k

k k k k k k k k

kind keen mink cake coke

kind keen mink cake coke

kick hike think chunk thank

kick hike think chunk thank

l

'l' goes up and around at the top red line like the 'h' and the 'k'. It comes down and curves around at the bottom blue line, finishing with an up-stroke to the top blue line.

l l l l l l l l l l

l l l l l l l l l l

l l l l l l l l l l

luck   kill   call   like   hulk

luck   kill   call   like   hulk

hold   heel   look   talk   lake

hold   heel   look   talk   lake

12

b

Checklist
Sit up straight ☐
Don't grip your pen too tightly ☐
Keep your writing forearm on the desk ☐

b b b b b b b b b b

b b b b b b b b b b

b b b b b b b b

bill   table   nibble   blank   bib

bill   table   nibble   blank   bib

black   bubble   bullet   ball   hob

black   bubble   bullet   ball   hob

h k l b

chat   kettle   blink   cook   double

chat   kettle   blink   cook   double

block   buckle   handle   knock

block   buckle   handle   knock

climb   bulb   quilt   tall   check

climb   bulb   quilt   tall   check

14

j

j *j* *j* *j* *j* *j* *j* *j* *j* *j*

j *j* *j* *j* *j* *j* *j* *j*

j *j* *j* *j* *j* *j* *j*

jack *jumble* *joined* *jab* *jet*

jack *jumble* *joined* *jab* *jet*

juice *joint* *jacket* *jail* *jam*

juice *joint* *jacket* *jail* *jam*

15

'g' begins like an 'a' but carries on straight down to form a loop at the bottom red line. It comes up to the top blue line, crossing the down-stroke at the bottom blue line.

g g g g g g g g g g

g g g g g g g g g

g g g g g g g g

juggle giggle judge huge log

juggle giggle judge huge log

bulge hang gong bang gun

bulge hang gong bang gun

16

y   y   y   y   y   y   y   y   y   y

y   y   y   y   y   y   y   y   y

y   y   y   y   y   y   y   y   y

buggy   ugly   yacht   young   day

buggy   ugly   yacht   young   day

handy quickly holly yell you

handy quickly holly yell you

'f' begins like 'h' but the down-stroke carries on down and around to form a loop at the bottom red line. It comes up and in between the two blue lines. It then goes up to the top blue line.

f   f   f

fill   fuel   loft   huff   bluff

lift   gift   funny   flat   fold

fe

Join from 'f' to 'e'
The join from 'f' circles down
and around at the top blue line
to make a loop for the 'e'.

Checklist
Sit up straight ☐
Don't grip your pen too tightly ☐
Keep your writing forearm on the desk ☐

fe fe fe fe fe fe fe fe fe fe

fe fe fe fe fe fe fe fe fe

fe fe fe fe fe fe fe fe

fell   toffee   feeble   fetch   life

feed fence feet fee female

19

'v' is made like a 'u' but finishes with a little curved line along the top blue line.

Checklist
Sit up straight ☐
Don't grip your pen too tightly ☐
Keep your writing forearm on the desk ☐

v v v v v v v v v v

v v v v v v v v v v

v v v v v v v v v v

voice van voyage having vote

voice van voyage having vote

value vacant victim violent

value vacant victim violent

20

'w' also finishes with a little curved line along the top blue line. When a word finishes with v, b, w or o, the curved line must also be made.

w w w w w w w w w w

w w w w w w w w w w

w w w w w w w w w w

when away jaw walk claw

when away jaw walk claw

view dew wife cow now

view dew wife cow now

ve we oe be

Join from v, w, o and b to e
When 'e' follows v, w, o or b, the join curves down to the middle of the two blue lines. It then goes up and around at the top blue line, making a loop for the 'e'.

ve ve ve we we we oe oe be

ve ve ve we we we oe oe be

ve ve ve we we we oe oe be

oven velvet weave between hoe

oven velvet weave between hoe

value venom went cove bet

value venom went cove bet

$\mathcal{N}$

The up-stroke goes a little above the top blue line. It comes back down and across a little way on the top blue line, before going down to the lower blue line and up to the top blue line.

$\mathcal{N}$ $\mathcal{N}$ $\mathcal{N}$ $\mathcal{N}$ $\mathcal{N}$ $\mathcal{N}$ $\mathcal{N}$ $\mathcal{N}$ $\mathcal{N}$ $\mathcal{N}$

$\mathcal{N}$ $\mathcal{N}$ $\mathcal{N}$ $\mathcal{N}$ $\mathcal{N}$ $\mathcal{N}$ $\mathcal{N}$ $\mathcal{N}$ $\mathcal{N}$

$\mathcal{N}$ $\mathcal{N}$ $\mathcal{N}$ $\mathcal{N}$ $\mathcal{N}$ $\mathcal{N}$ $\mathcal{N}$ $\mathcal{N}$

hurry tram carry runner try

hurry tram carry runner try

where ever river furry harm

where ever river furry harm

or *br* *wr*

or *or* *or* *br* *br* *br* *wr* *wr* *wr*

or *or* *or* *br* *br* *br* *wr* *wr* *wr*

or *or* *or* *br* *br* *br* *wr* *wr* *wr*

wreck *border* *write* *bring* *for*

wreck *border* *write* *bring* *for*

born *wrong* *organ* *more* *corn*

born *wrong* *organ* *more* *corn*

h k l b f

wife   why   ferry   lorry   work

wife   why   ferry   lorry   work

grief   coffee   voyage   barge   drink

grief   coffee   voyage   barge   drink

lucky   dribble   drive   crab   king

lucky   dribble   drive   crab   king

25

s s s s s s s s s s

s s s s s s s s s

s s s s s s s s s

shore lesson brass stars ask

shore lesson brass stars ask

storm fast straws sobs snow

storm fast straws sobs snow

The up-stroke goes to the top blue line and then up halfway between the top blue line and the top red line. It comes down again to the halfway mark between the bottom blue line and the bottom red line. It then comes up to finish like 'n'.

p p p p p p p p p p p
p p p p p p p p p p p
p p p p p p p p p p

pepper puppy paper pump up

pepper puppy paper pump up

spend past happy pink post

spend past happy pink post

Checklist

Sit up straight ☐
Don't grip your pen too tightly ☐
Keep your writing forearm on the desk ☐

The up-stroke goes up and around at the top blue line. The letter is made like a '3'. It finishes with an up-stroke to the top blue line.

z z z z z z z z z z z

z z z z z z z z z z z

z z z z z z z z z z z

puzzle   dazzle   zebra   quiz   zoo

puzzle   dazzle   zebra   quiz   zoo

zigzag   zero   zoom   zipper

zigzag   zero   zoom   zipper

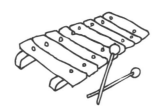

The up-stroke curves around at the top blue line and goes down diagonally, curving at the bottom blue line and up to the top blue line. The word is finished before making the backward cross on 'x' which is at numeral '2'.

N *N* *N* *N* *N* *N* *N* *N* *N* *N*

N *N* *N* *N* *N* *N* *N* *N* *N*

N *N* *N* *N* *N* *N* *N* *N*

boxes   fixes   tax   vixen   fox

oxygen   next   xylophone   ox

Practice

Now you know how to join all your letters. We practise all the letters again when we write these words. Write the whole word before dotting the 'i' and 'j' and finishing 'x' with the backward cross.

floor kitchen gate junk park

floor kitchen gate junk park

basket voice untie divide crew

basket voice untie divide crew

quick year hammer strong law

quick year hammer strong law

Practice

circle square triangle rectangle

circle square triangle rectangle

add subtract multiply divide

add subtract multiply divide

jacket jumper shirt dress top

jacket jumper shirt dress top

Capital Letters

Now we begin to write our capital letters. These ten capital letters are formed just like the lowercase letters.

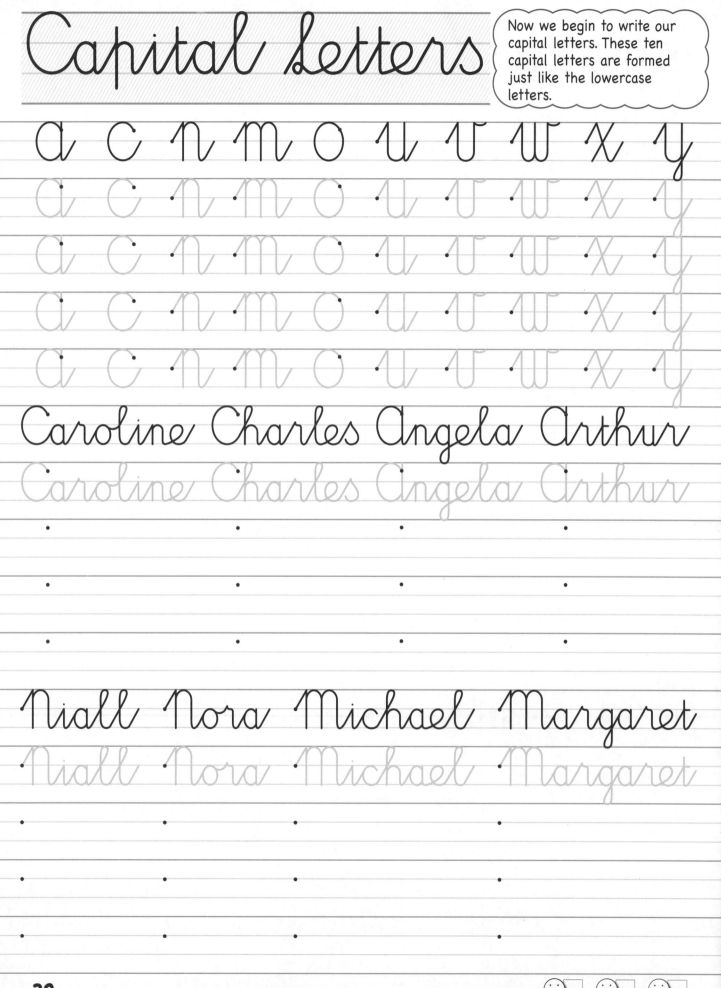

A C N M O U V W X Y

Caroline Charles Angela Arthur

Niall Nora Michael Margaret

Capital Letters

Don't forget to finish the word before dotting the 'i', crossing the 't' and making the backward stroke on the 'x'.

Ursula   Ultan   Oliver   Orla

Vincent   Veronica   William   Wilma

Xavier   Xanthe   Yvonne   Yvette

T T

'T' and 'F' are formed in the same way. The pencil has to be lifted to cross the 'F' where the numeral '2' is.

T   T   T   T   T   T   T   T

T   T   T   T   T   T   T   T

Thomas   Terry   Teresa   Timothy

Thomas   Terry   Teresa   Timothy

F   F   F   F   F   F   F   F

F   F   F   F   F   F   F   F

F   F   F   F   F   F   F   F

Frank   Fiona   Fergus   Fidelma

Frank   Fiona   Fergus   Fidelma

‹I› and ‹J› begin at the top blue line. The ‹J› begins like an ‹I› but goes down to the bottom red line and around to form a loop. The up-stroke on the ‹J› crosses the down-stroke on the bottom blue line.

Ivor   Ita   Ignatius   Ivan

Jack   Jacinta   Jennifer   Judy

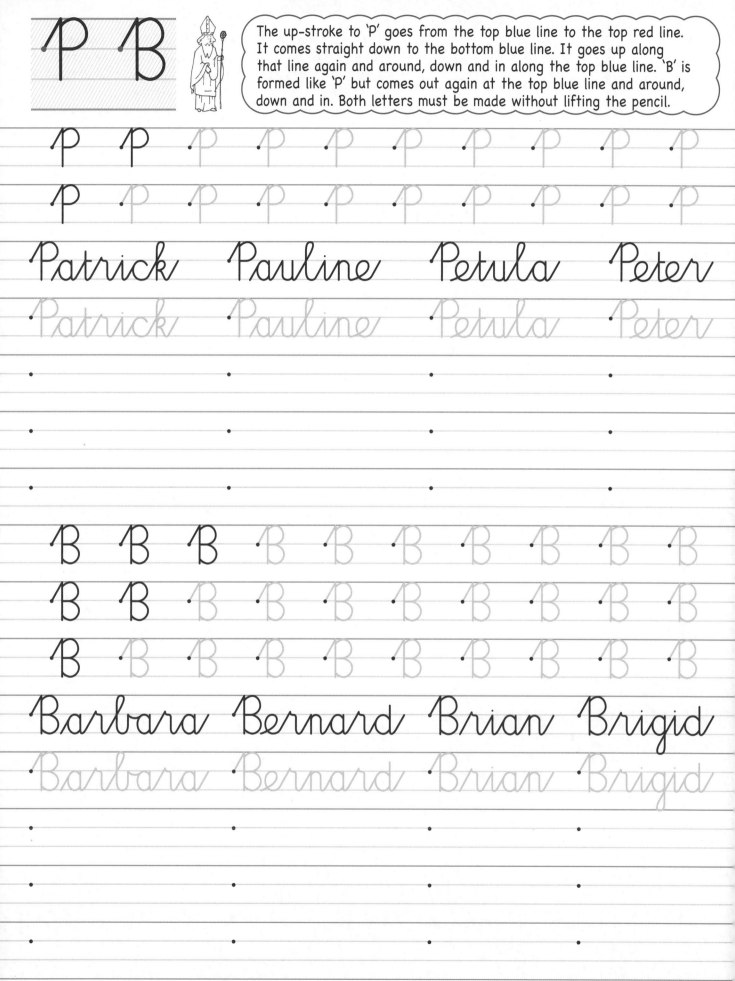

The up-stroke to 'P' goes from the top blue line to the top red line. It comes straight down to the bottom blue line. It goes up along that line again and around, down and in along the top blue line. 'B' is formed like 'P' but comes out again at the top blue line and around, down and in. Both letters must be made without lifting the pencil.

P P P P P P P P P P

P P P P P P P P P P

Patrick   Pauline   Petula   Peter

Patrick   Pauline   Petula   Peter

B B B B B B B B B B

B B B B B B B B B B

B B B B B B B B B B

Barbara   Bernard   Brian   Brigid

Barbara   Bernard   Brian   Brigid

R D

'R' begins like 'P' and 'B' but comes out at the top blue line, around and down to the bottom blue line and up to the top blue line. 'D' begins a little way down from the top red line, comes out in a curved line at the bottom blue line and goes up and around at the top red line.

R R R R R R R R R R

R R R R R R R R R

R R R R R R R R R

Rory   Rita   Robert   Rebecca

Rory   Rita   Robert   Rebecca

D D D D D D D D D D

D D D D D D D D D

Derek   Deirdre   Desmond   Dora

Derek   Deirdre   Desmond   Dora

L L G

L L L L L L L L L L L
L L L L L L L L L L L
L L L L L L L L L L L

Larry   Laura   Liam   Linda
Larry   Laura   Liam   Linda

G G G G G G G G G G G
G
Gary   Gertrude   Gwen   Gina
Gary   Gertrude   Gwen   Gina

38

𝒮 𝒮 𝒮 𝒮 𝒮 𝒮 𝒮 𝒮 𝒮

𝒮 𝒮 𝒮 𝒮 𝒮 𝒮 𝒮 𝒮 𝒮

Sally   Stephen   Susan   Stella

Sally   Stephen   Susan   Stella

ℰ ℰ ℰ ℰ ℰ ℰ ℰ ℰ ℰ

ℰ ℰ ℰ ℰ ℰ ℰ ℰ ℰ ℰ

ℰ ℰ ℰ ℰ ℰ ℰ ℰ ℰ ℰ

Eamonn   Eileen   Enda   Emily

Eamonn   Eileen   Enda   Emily

Z Q

'z' makes a wavy line along the top red line, comes back down to the bottom blue line and makes another wavy line along the bottom blue line. 'Q' is made like 'O'. The pencil has to be lifted to make the tail for the 'Q' at numeral '2'.

Z Z Z Z Z Z Z Z Z Z Z

Z Z Z Z Z Z Z Z Z Z Z

Zachary   Zelda   Zelma   Zoe

Q Q Q Q Q Q Q Q Q Q Q

Q Q Q Q Q Q Q Q Q Q Q

Q Q Q Q Q Q Q Q Q Q Q

Queenie Quentin Queenie Quentin

The pencil has to be lifted to finish these two letters. The numeral '2' shows you where the pencil is placed to finish the letters. 'K' and 'H' each have a straight line down to the bottom blue line. To finish 'H', the pencil comes down straight to the bottom blue line, curves back around to form a loop at the top blue line and finishes at the top blue line.

K K K K K K K K K K

K K K K K K K K K K

Kathleen   Kevin   Keith   Kitty

Kathleen   Kevin   Keith   Kitty

H H H H H H H H H H H

H H H H H H H H H H H

H H H H H H H H H H H

Henry   Hazel   Howard   Hugh

Henry   Hazel   Howard   Hugh

Practice

We practise writing the capital and the lowercase letters again when we write these sentences.

Can Colm carry the cat?

Can

Angela and Art are in America.

Angela

Victor's violin is very valuable.

Victor's

When did William go to Wales?

When

Jack joined judo class in July.

Jack

Practice

The up-stroke for 'G' goes from the bottom blue line.

Roger repaired Rory's red racer.

Roger

Quickly, said Mr O'Donoghue.

Quickly

Kitty the kangaroo kicked Ken.

Kitty

'Bring Betty back', said Ben.

Bring

Gregory gave Glenda the goggles.

Gregory

Proverbs

Rome wasn't built in a day.

Rome .

Two heads are better than one.

Two .

It's better to be safe than sorry.

It's .

It pays to pay attention.

It .

Many hands make light work.

Many .

Facts

There is no up-stroke to capital 'A'.

Dublin Zoo is in Phoenix Park.

Dublin

The Manx cat has no tail.

The

A cygnet is a young swan.

A

Ballina is in North Mayo.

Ballina

A wasp can sting several times.

A

Facts

Remember: There is no up-stroke from 's' when it is the last letter in a word.

Bees collect pollen from flowers.

Bees

Leitrim has the shortest coastline.

Leitrim

Deciduous trees shed their leaves.

Deciduous

A spider has eight legs.

A spider has eight legs

Some animals hibernate in winter.

Some

Proverbs

Learn to walk before you run.

Learn

Money cannot buy everything.

Money

The more haste, the less speed.

The

Well begun is half done.

Well

One good turn deserves another.

One

Relations

Now that you have finished the book, you should be very pleased with your writing!

brother   sister   son   daughter

brother

nephew   niece   uncle   aunt

nephew

parents children family relation

parents